Christians Are People Too!

A Reflection Through Skits

Venasta D. Parsons

TaylorMade Publishing
www.taylormadepublishing.com
904-323-1334

Unless otherwise indicated, all scripture references are from
King James Version (KJV)
New King James Version (NKJV)

Christians Are People Too, A Reflection Through Skits

Copyright © October 2020 by Venasta D. Parsons.
All rights reserved
ISBN: 978-0-9968123-8-2

This book or parts thereof may not be reproduced in any form, stored in a retrieval system, or transmitted in any form by any means; electronic, mechanical, photocopy, recording, or otherwise-without prior written permission of the publisher, except as provided by United States of America copyright.

For more information and additional copies:
Venasta Parsons
Email: venasta.thomas92@gmail.com
Or contact www.taylormadepublishingfl.com

Table of Contents

Introduction 1
Who Are You? 2
An Unexpected Visitation 9
Battle of the Spouses... 17
About My Father's Business.. 21
Jesus Birth in our Technology World!..27
Staying in Your, Lane Keeps you Sane 42
About the Author 43

Introduction

Living in Hinesville, Ga for 18 years, I spent time daily journaling as part of my normal routine. As a member of a terrific church I would get inspired by the Holy Spirit to write skits about how a Christian would truly deal with a given situation when no one was watching. I was blessed to write a skit every year for five years!

When I shared them with my pastors, they were excited and allowed me to share them during our New Year's Eve services! As I would write the skit, I could actually see the people from my church family that would fit each role/character perfectly! Everyone I asked to participate did so with much support and enthusiasm! This continued for five years straight; people would ask me each year if I had a skit to perform, it was so phenomenal!

For each play or skit written I would place myself in each role, pondering what I would actually say and do if no one else could see and hear me but God! Most of the time I would respond out of my emotions and of course say it over in my mind and speak it out loud. Writing it all down was the final decision.

This is how the birthing of "Christians Are People Too", entered the book world. Jesus Birth in our Technology world was written to imagine just how it could be today with our multimedia/electronic universe. May these skits be a blessing to all readers and for those who decide to perform them, I salute you and I thank you!

Who Are You?

Cast of Characters

Narrator..
Dr. Luke...............................Married, successful with 3 kids
Mrs. MeMe Richly....................Married business owner
Justina Washington.................Single mother (of twins)
Angel Justice..........................Graduate Scholar
Grace Bishop.........................Single, court stenographer

Scriptural References	Props/Items
Matthew 12:34	Microphones, Desk with 2 Chairs, Large Bible, Hand Mirror, Laptop, Computer, or Tablet, Photo of each character, Gavel, Bottle of Anointing Oil, Recording of a cell phone ringing, basket of laundry, bowl, and spoon (cell phone playing worship music-scene 5) Example Pandora Music or YouTube
Proverbs 16:18	
Matthew 4:31-32	
Matthew 7:5	
Mark 10:25	

Scene 1

Narrator:

Dr. Luke is sitting in his office admiring his accomplishments! He just came off an 18-hour shift in labor & delivery department; let's listen to his conversation with the Lord.

Dr. Luke:

Whew Lord I am bushed! I am getting tired of all these women having babies! Whatever happened to birth control? Oh, don't get me wrong Lord, I am thankful for my three kids, but I will never have another one. It sure does feel good being the top obstetrician in the state. (*Looks in the mirror, raises arms up in victory*) If you need your baby delivered, call me, C-section, no problem, twins connected at the hip, head, back hurry up & call me! The legendary Dr. Luke!

Oh Lord who am I fooling? I'm tired of this life; I want to spend more time with my family! I want to go fishing, I want to take that 7-day vacation to Paris, I want a pay increase so I can buy that 80ft Carver yacht and give $50 to the church mission's fund. I meant to thank you for the sports car I was able to buy for my wife, and I will give $100 to the pastor's 8-year church anniversary. Well thanks for listening Lord and thanks again for all the wonderful blessings I have. (*Lights out*)

Scene 2

Narrator:
Mrs. MeMe Richly is a top-notch catering businesswoman in Jacksonville, FL. She hosts parties for the Mayor, Senator and Governor twice a year which gives her full exposure to the elite class of citizens. Her husband is a humble man who runs a prosperous janitorial service for several hospital clinics and two prominent lawyers. Matthew 12:34 tells us that out of the abundance of the heart the mouth speaks, let's hear her heart today.

MeMe: (*Sitting down and cell phone rings*)
Hello girl! I am too tired to blink my eyes right now. That Mayor's party was 10 hours long; setup started at 8 AM and I didn't even have dessert. Oh, girl my husband will be ok, I can't believe he had the nerve to call me and...Haaa oh heck no he better not even think to ask me for that! No, he asked what I was cooking for dinner; I could've smacked his face twice! He better pick-up a Pizza Hut! He can have one of his 10 employees to get him Piccadilly's. I am not his waitress. Huh? Pray for him? He better pray for himself.

Oh, of course I'll be at Sunday night service, since they only have it once a month, I guess I can record Cold Case because it comes on at 9pm and I know somebody is gonna do a long drawn out prayer! Why are they having this marriage enrichment anyway? Most of them have good husbands, not a pain in the butt like mine. I better hang up before I get in the flesh, don't go spreading my business, I trust you girl, Amen see ya later, God bless you!! (*Lights out*)

Scene 3

Narrator:
Success can be extremely dangerous when we don't know how to receive it humbly and wisely. It is written in Proverbs 16:18 "Pride goeth before destruction and a haughty spirit before a fall." Listen to the prideful Angel Justice, a 25-year old law student, who graduated with the highest GPA ever recorded, Life is all about her...or is it? How fast will her fall be? How hard will it be?

Angel: (*Stands up looking at herself in the mirror, holding gold diploma in one hand, blowing kisses to herself*)

Girl, you are the most intelligent woman in the universe! You are so, so smart with your 5.8 GPA! Brains and beauty do go together well! I am going to be the most influential judge in this state, shoot in this world! Move over Judge Judy, lookout Judge Hatchett, and Judge Tolbert has nothing on me, they may be on TV. But I'm going national! The honorable, classy Judge Angel Justice has arrived. (*Sits down in the chair, places the mirror, diploma on the table*)

Lord, I want to thank you for making me smarter than everyone I know, and those I don't know. I've worked hard for this prestigious title; I am the youngest female in history to achieve this honor. My name will be on everyone's lips for the next 50 years! Thank you, Lord, (*lifts up small bag with white sugar*) this little powder never hurts me, just makes me smarter! No police officer, no sheriff, no lawyer can ever touch me, I am too important to my city, this state, and the whole world. (*Picks up gavel*) I can do what I want, when I want, and how I choose! I am the honorable, anointed, appointed and approved Judge Angel Justice! Amen, (*slams gravel on the table twice. Lights out*)

Scene 4

Narrator:

Life for Justina Washington a 30-year-old single mother of twin girls is a simple, lonely, and frustrating one. Her five-year-old twin daughters demands a lot of her time. Her husband divorced her when he found out she was having twins! Justina has no social life; her focus is on her girls, bank teller job and church. It's strange that her mother is her closest friend! Let's hear how she sees her perspective on life. Maybe you will hear some bitterness! Maybe even some anger!

Justina: (*Dressed with rollers in hair, jogging suit and eating a bowl of ice cream, phone rings*)

Hello mom, yes ma'am I am doing good, no the girls are asleep. Mom please don't start up with the dating talk, I am not interested in anyone but my girls! They're my life and...yes, I know that God is a jealous God, I give Him some time too. I pray every morning before leaving for work, I pray every night before going to bed and before I eat! There's only so much prayer a person can do, everyone is not like you mom!! I'm sorry; I'm just sleepy right now. (*Puts the phone down and responds with yes, yes I know*) I know I'm getting older and so are the girls!

(*Picks phone back up*) Mom please stop saying that I hate men, I don't, just one man, DJ, their father. You're right mom, all men are not pigs, snakes or dogs; and you and dad are blessed to have such an awesome marriage for 45 years, Yippee, (*holds the phone in the air away from her ears*) I did join a church two months ago, the girls love the children's church but I don't trust any of them yet. Well I gotta go now, good night, love you! Lord will you please send me a husband so my mother will stay out of my life and quit bugging me?

God can you let him be handsome, rich, and a praying man too! I promise I will cook, clean, even wash his car. In the bedroom I will not hold back, but give him what he needs, when he needs it, well unless my favorite show is on; "five minutes lottery numbers bingo"! Because you know I follow that every Thursday at 10pm, I only play with $5.00. Oh Lord, I once read somewhere in the Bible that it's better to marry than to burn, I don't know what that means but I don't want it to be me! Wait a minute what am I saying? I have a great job, a nice home, a decent car, so having a husband isn't all that anyway! Men are just spoiled; selfish jerks and no man better say one word to me about doing anything! Or going anywhere! In Jesus name I pray Amen.

Scene 5

Narrator:
Grace Bishop is a 50-year-old single woman with no children, never been married! A born again, sanctified Christian for 40 years, a powerful prayer warrior, and dresses in the full armor of God every morning at 3:15 am; a Bible scholar, faithfully dedicated, loyal, and committed to her church. She knows everything about everybody at her church! And even knows everyone by name, honest with everyone except to herself, Bible toting, scriptural quoting virtuous woman or not? Let's find out.

Grace: (*Sitting at table with each picture of the characters, open bottle of oil and on the table, Bible open, sets praise and worship music, lifts up hands towards heaven and begins*)

Father oh Father, I come to you most holy God in the name of Jesus! I have some people here who need your great intervention, or they will be utterly destroyed. Save them, set them free and deliver them!

(*Holds up photo of Dr. Luke, anoints it with oil*) Lord this is a greedy selfish man and his heart is not turned to you. Show him the truth about himself and make him give more to the church, he's rich for a reason. Mark 10:25 says it's easier for a camel to pass through the eye of a needle than for him to enter the Kingdom of God, In Jesus name Amen

(*Holds up photo of MeMe and anoints it with oil*) Lord please shut her gossiping mouth! Her tongue is poison and she cuts her husband down all the time. He's only been to service twice in 4 years, and we all know why he doesn't come. Make her thankful for that man and I pray he doesn't beat her down or divorce her, but if he did it would be funny! Tame her tongue, Matthew 12:34 says out of the abundance of the heart the mouth speaks, in Jesus name Amen.

(*Holds up picture of Angel, anoints it with oil, prays in tongues*) Now Lord this child needs some serious deliverance, she's on drugs and she don't fool me. Keep her from going to jail, she's so pretty and intelligent, she wouldn't last four hours in prison! Send angels to shake and awake her before we see her on the headline news! I bind that deceptive spirit in Jesus Name!

(*Holds up photo of Justina, pours a lot of oil on it*) Lord that girl needs a husband! May you cover her and those sweet little darling twins, I just pray they don't act and talk smart like their mother! Make her soften her words because I almost slapped her last Sunday for the way she talked me! Here lately I've come close to slapping some of these foolish women! They better be glad I'm saved, sanctified and Holy Ghost filled! You saw how that heifer acted and heard what she said when I turned to hold the door open for her, she said, "I don't need your help lady I got it" now you know I was ready to slap her then! Jesus Jesus (*shakes her head and just slams her photo on the table*)

Lord Bless our pastor and his wife and their whole family. Bless our congregation and please please don't let the choir sing that song "SHOUT" I'm so tired of that song. Thank you, Lord,!

Narrator:
So, we see that people do have areas of their lives where help is needed. Some of our sinful ways are not as exposed as others, but the grace of God is still available! He wants your identity to be hidden in Him, no one else or nothing else! Something we need to consider before leaving...I didn't die on that cross for you! And you didn't die on that cross for me so that settles it! I dare you to read Matthew 7:5 Amen.
(*Lights out--Introduce the cast*)

An Unexpected Visitation

Cast of Characters

Narrator	Male/Female voice
Pastor	Pastor Comfort
Pastor's Wife	Sister Comfort
Rich Man	Gary Estate
Rich Man's wife	Naomi Estate (voice only)
Secretary	April Perfect
Husband & Wife	Mr. & Mrs. Harmony
Harmony twins	Zion & Joy (boy & girl) voices only reading their letter
Scene 1	Pastor @ Pulpit
Scene 2	Gary Estate's office
Scene 3	Couple sitting in Den
Scene 4	Pastor @ Pulpit

Scriptural References	Props/Items
Matthew 24:6-22 MSG Mark 13:19-20 MSG 1 Timothy 4:1 MSG	- Telephone/cell phone - Laptop, 2 chairs, desk, 4 chairs, table - Large Bible - Microphones, overhead and 2 handheld/attached - Name of Church, Midnight Cry Baptist Church

Scene 1

Narrator:

The pastor is standing in front of the congregation and welcomes everyone to Midnight Cry Baptist Church, wonder what he's sharing today.

Pastor:

Good morning body of Christ! I pray that all is well with you, your family, and friends oh yes, even your enemies too, remember, they to have a soul, Amen. As I stand here before

you on this supernatural Sunday, I want you to know that my wife, Sis Comfort is still at the women's "Don't be left behind" conference in Stillwater, Florida and should be returning early on Miracle Monday, Yes, thank you Jesus!
I sure do miss her. *(shakes his head and closes his eyes for a minute)* Please know that all visitors are welcome today and loved by the Midnight Cry Church family. Open your Bible to Matthew 24:6-22, write down, Mark 13:19 & 20, because I'll include it also lastly we'll visit 1 Timothy 4:1, I'll give you a few minutes to read it quietly, for yourself, while the music plays.

I have been impressed by the Holy Spirit to just talk to you a little and shine the light on Christ's return. Now we are going to explore the persecution of the Christians, in these last days we're living in, plus how we will be tested and tried prior to the coming of the Lord.

The tribulation period, which is coming, will be severe, and unfortunately many will fall away from the faith! I pray that it won't be any one of us, *(makes a circle with his finger and ends up pointing to himself)*.

We see in the word of God that one day Jesus will return for his bride! Amen, His coming will break the back of the tribulation period. We must have our hearts and minds prepared for being a true Christian! It will require the utmost commitment and endurance. If not, we too will turn and run quickly from the faith!

This morning as we prepare to leave, let's pray to God for His Dunamis power to reign in us, over us strengthening us with endurance to stand! Be encouraged body of Christ! Jesus is coming again; See some of you Wednesday night...hopefully! And see others of you on Sunday maybe! *(Lights out)*

Scene 2

Narrator:
We see the rich businessman, Mr. Estate, a licensed architect, owner of "Lavish Living Construction Company" sitting in his million-dollar building, which he designed! Wonder what's going on in his world today, let's listen.

Mr. Estate: (*Sounds irate and talks loudly*)
Mrs. Perfect get in here now! I need to know what is going on with the computer system. I can't dial out on my phone line, both of my top men, Joshua & Caleb were in the final sign off meeting with the president of Canaan Corporation and the live feed just blacked out. Get me some answers now!

Mrs. Perfect: (*Runs into his office with her tablet and headphones*)
Yes Sir Mr. Estate I'm trying to read the news report flashing up now! It says here that two men were arrested at Canaan Corporation due to a violent fight in a meeting...oh my goodness it's Joshua & Caleb!! (*Holds the tablet up for him to see*)

Mr. Estate
What in the world? I want some answers now!

Mrs. Perfect: (*continues watching her tablet*)
Well they are saying something about Joshua and Caleb prayed over a contract and used the words, "In Jesus Name" which sparked anger with the president and when Joshua and Caleb said that they were Christians and always pray over contracts, that's when the president jumped on them, hitting them both in the face, oh wow!

Mr. Estate:
That's ridiculous, we've always prayed over our contracts and ended with saying, "In Jesus Name" It's our foundational principle and everyone knows that.

Mrs. Perfect: (*Starts shaking her head and reads*)
Oh, my goodness the breaking news is flashing! Anyone using, "In Jesus Name" will be arrested and if found to be a Christian they will be charged with subversive actions which carries a death sentence! This is crazy we Christians are not trying to overthrow anything!

Mr. Estate: (*Drops down in his chair shaking his head, and sobs*)
My wife is a real Christian, she's handling the papers for the Galatians Library building contract, I wonder if she'll be arrested.

Mrs. Perfect:
E-mails are pouring in from all over, faxes are going crazy, phone lines are tied, I'm not able to send out any messages, but still receiving the breaking news! This is chaos, (*runs out crying*)

Mr. Estate: (*Rubbing his head, talks to himself*)
I just don't understand it, what's happening? Oh my, Naomi, how's my Naomi? (*Calls for secretary*) Hey please check and see if my wife left any messages earlier today, it's our 30th wedding anniversary and I forgot to order flowers! But I did leave something special under her pillow. Oh man, Father God please help me!

Mrs. Perfect: (*Enters the office holding up email*)
(*Mr. Estate looks at her and shakes his head*) ...read it please, read it.

Naomi: (*voice*)

Happy Anniversary darling, I love you so much. Guess what I found under my pillow? Oh, Gary, you shouldn't have! It must be 5 carats! It's stunningly beautiful and I'll wear it for all eternity, I love you forever! And ever! Life is amazing being married to you these 30 yrs, it feels so good knowing you've finally considered becoming a true Christian, letting go of that religious crap, ok I won't preach to you but Jesus loves you more than I ever could, see you tonight at 6 sharp, intercessory prayer is over at 5, no grandkids just you & me baby!!

Mr. Estate:

Oh my goodness, there she goes with that Christian stuff, I believe in God and I don't have to read the Bible everyday to prove it, plus I pray every Sunday, gee what more does she want? I am thinking about praying on Wednesdays too since most churches have services then, that'll be fine with me. Mrs. Perfect call Naomi's church, I want to speak with her pastor!

Scene 3

Narrator:

Mr. & Mrs. Harmony are relaxing at home, they both are grateful for their job promotions and excited that their twins are doing so well in school. The twins are turning 13 next week! Let's listen in on the proud couple.

Mr. Harmony

Ooo-ooo-weeeee, man I am tired! This was a long week and I can't wait to start morning shift next week. I'm happy baby, nobody but God did it, to think I was the only one promoted to first shift permanently. Honey those prayers of yours really work. It was rough doing night shift for $25 an hour but now, day shift at $20 it really isn't a hard cut.

Mrs. Harmony:
That's right honey; the Lord knew we needed that pay, since the twins are growing so fast it's getting expensive to keep them in all the name brand clothes and sneakers. I'm thankful for my part time job at Dillard's, $10 an hour isn't bad plus I get great employee discounts, every penny counts, Amen! (*they give each other a high five*)

Mr. Harmony:
It's just a little sad that I will be working three Sundays a month, which makes me available for church only once a month. I wonder what the church folk gonna think.

Mrs. Harmony: (*Holding two letters in her hand*)
Honey, we haven't opened these two letters from the twins table, they put them out two days ago, and I bet they wrote a nice thank you for those brand new Fendi (*pronounced fendee*) sneakers. Hey this first letter is from your job; (*opening it and reads silently*) oh no, no, no this is a joke! Honey it says that your position is terminated, and the promotion is going to someone else, please accept this severance check for $20,000 and your final papers explaining your termination for religious practices on the job, can be picked up Monday, thank you!

Mr. Harmony:
That's insane; I don't know what they're talking about! All I do is pray every morning when I get to my station and sometimes, I do anoint the desk with oil, but I have never bothered anyone. Oh, I always end my prayers with, "In Jesus Name" maybe I should have just used my own name huh? Lol.

Mrs. Harmony:
Honey this isn't funny what are we gonna do? I guess I need to call the church intercessory prayer line to start the prayers! Oh

well God sees it. Maybe this other letter has better news, here you open it.

Mr. Harmony:
What is going on? (*Letter is read in Zion's voice*) Dear mom & dad we know you are finding this letter way late because you guys sleep in late on weekends. Joy and I are at Ms. CeCe's church to help pass out water to the people on the "Jesus Saves" 5 mile run at the main park. They invited us last month but when we tried to talk to you about it you said you were tired and will discuss it later.

(*Joy's voice*) ...Please don't be mad at us, we called a taxi to take us there, he knows us and his name is Mr. Moses, he will bring us back home. Remember how you always tell us that angels are with us everywhere we go, well they will be with us while we're out, plus Ms. CeCe keeps us close to her whenever we go to the children's sanctuary, we know she's gonna take us under her wings. We should be home by 6pm unless Jesus comes back first, just like grandma always says, we love you both okay. (*Lights out*)

Scene 4

Pastor:
It's quite a joy to see everyone for wonderful Wednesday night Bible study! I will only be before you for 45 minutes, we've had some shocking events take place at the beginning of the week, so I will share them with you, we will pray about it and go home in peace!

Y'all excuse me for a minute while I give God praise for bringing Mrs. Comfort back home safely! She's one of the reasons we are getting out of here early, Amen!!

Well, it is with great concern that some of our members have been arrested! I received a call last night that, Deacons; Shadrach, Meshach and Abednego were taken to the county jail, now I haven't seen them yet, but they sounded ok and told me that they're gonna have deliverance service while in there, y'all know how they are!! So just keep them in prayer. We know God hears and answers us, Amen.

Sis Comfort: (*stands beside her husband rubbing his shoulder smiling*)
I just want to say how blessed it is to be back in the house of the Lord, and home with my "teddy bear" I mean pastor Comfort y'all have to excuse me today, (laughing) But on the serious side, Pray much for Still Waters Florida, the city was posting up warning signs about using "In Jesus Name" out in public! It felt like being a Christian is the worst thing in the world.

I felt in my spirit that something huge is coming, so I just want to encourage you with this little saying, "No intimidations, no manipulations and no dominations will control me! Not from the world, not my flesh, or the devil" AMEN!

Pastor Comfort:
As we stand and prepare to leave, I will say to you all, today is the day to settle your heart and know that on Christ the solid rock we stand, all other ground is sinking sand! Tomorrow things could change, and we don't want to be uncertain, unknowing, or unsaved!! Think about this before you go to bed tonight; "what will your last words be?"
(*Lights out!*)

Battle of the Spouses

(*Use the couple's real first & last names*)
Couple One..................................Mr. & Mrs. _____
Couple Two..................................Mr. & Mrs. _____
Couple Three................................Mr. & Mrs. _____
Couple Four..................................Mr. & Mrs. _____
Game show Host.........................Mr. Amos Quizzley
Narrator (*Keeps the points for each couple*)

Props/Items
<ul><li>Answers will be written down on poster boards (16 needed) in black marker for the wives and red marker for the husbands.</li><li>Scores are calculated by five points for each matching answer.</li><li>The two bonus questions will be worth 15 points each. Couple with the most points wins!!</li><li>8 chairs with each couple sitting back to back of each other, begin with all the women facing the front</li></ul>

Narrator/Game shows host:
Three couples will receive a complimentary $250.00 gift card to Ruth's Chris Steak House. The winning couple receives an all expenses paid 5-day, 4-night Romantic getaway to… The Breakers Resort, West Palm Beach FL. American Airlines will fly you round trip first class! Enjoy the nice beaches, top European spa, fine dining, and smooth jazz nights! Comes With all meals included! One bottle of champagne and one bottle of Moscato Wine will await you in your deluxe honeymoon suite at the 5-star Breakers Resort!

Mr. Amos Quizzley: (*Introduces each couple by saying hello!*) Each couple has been married for 12-18 months; let's see how well they know each other. Let's go!

Couple One (first names only)
Couple Two (first names only)
Couple Three (first names only)
Couple Four (first names only)

Wives will write their answers on poster boards and after 2 minutes the fun begins! Questions will be repeated twice; husbands answer first then wives show what they have written on their card!

Question #1. What animal describes your husband's attitude when you're out in public? Silly as a monkey, quiet as a mouse, or loud like a lion

Question #2. Where's your husband's best place to cuddle? The beach, the fireplace, the bedroom, or the Living room?

Question #3. What color was your husband wearing on your first date?

Question #4. How many chores are listed on your "honey do" list?

Question #5. How many chores are completed?

Question #6. What are your husband's most comfortable clothes? Jeans, shorts, or pjs

Question #7. Who is the better cook you or him?

Question #8. Bonus question: What is your husband's favorite sport? Basketball, baseball, football, hockey or fishing? Must be one of these!

Part One

(*The husbands are asked questions and the wives use their written answers on the card while the husbands speak their answer! Point system remains the same*)

Couple one-husband………………Wife shows her answer…Points?
Couple two-husband ………………Wife shows her answer…Points?
Couple three-husband……………Wife shows her answer…Points?
Couple four-husband………………Wife shows her answer…Points?

Part Two

(*Couples switch places*)

The wives are asked questions and the husbands use their written answers on the card while the wives speak their answer! Point system remains the same.

Couple one-wife…………………Husband shows his answer…Points?
Couple two-wife…………………Husband shows his answer…Points?
Couple three-wife………………Husband shows his answer Points?
Couple four-wife…………………Husband shows his answer…Points?

Question #1. If your husband could get rid of one thing of yours what would it be?

Question #2. What is your husband's most annoying habit that he does?

Question #3. How many times a day does your husband tell you that he loves you?

Question #4. How many times a day do you tell your husband that you love him?

Question #5. Who makes the loudest noise when you make whoopee?

Question #6. How many of your husbands' relatives do you really get along with?

Question #7. Since being married, how many times have you eaten out for dinner? Over 50 times or less than 50 times?

Question #8. Bonus question: What mode of transportation is your wife most likely to take for a 5-hour trip? Plane, train, motorcycle, ship or automobile (includes car, truck or SUV).

About My Father's Business

A look at Luke 2:41-51 and how it would look in 2020?

Cast of Characters:

Narrator	Mr. /Mrs. Voice
Mother	Sister Annie Joy
Father	Brother Larry Joy
Son	Billy Joy
Preacher	Pastor Frank
Deacon	Deacon Smith
Elder	Elder Moore
Evangelist	Evangelist Lovely
Man at Airport	Mr. Mannings

Props/items
- Microphones
- 4-suitcases
- Cell phones, 3 bottles of water
- 3 chairs side by side for airplane ride
- 3 rows of 5 chairs each for church lobby area, one table.
- Sound effects-airport, boarding & flight announcements.
- One chair where man is sitting in airport terminal with his suitcase, 3 headphones/earphones

---

Narrator:

Story begins with the Joy family planning a trip to Atlanta GA for a huge gathering of Spiritual leaders at Miracle Temple. They have a yearly gathering where the Baptist District 12 denomination leaders get together to encourage, engage, empower, and enrich each other with the Word of God! We will follow the Joys, a Christian family who has been blessed by God with an amazing 12-year-old son!! This is their very first year taking their son; they usually leave him with his grandparents but not this time!

SCENE 1

Annie:
(*Everyone leaving home heading to the airport*)
Is everyone all packed so we can get to the airport on time? I know you better have nice clean jeans, no holy socks or underwear!! Billy I am not playing!

Billy:
I am all packed mom and I have five pairs: ok we're only going to be there for the weekend!

Larry:
I guess that means I better have 5 clean pairs also!
(*Laughing at son*)

Billy:
I have those 3 bottles of water too, just in case!
(*Holds them up*)

Annie:
(*While taking luggage out of the room*)
Honey please set the alarm! Set the light timers! Unplug the coffee pot! Make sure the bedroom doors are closed and locked!

Larry:
(*looks up at the ceiling*)
My goodness Lord, this woman would remind you of what to do! Holy Spirit please help me to get through this weekend with a smile.

Billy:
(*smiles at his dad*)
He heard you! Don't worry I've got it covered!

SCENE 2

Narrator:
They get to the airport and get on the plane, while on the plane Billy has a window seat and stares out the window, waving his hands.

Annie:
Billy why are you waving we're up in the clouds, nobody can see you!

Billy:
(Replies, under his breath) Hmmm that's what she thinks...I'm waving to my Heavenly Father! He's with us you know!

Narrator:
Everyone puts on their headphones and continues the flight. They land in the Atlanta airport and Billy goes over to an elderly man to offer him 2 bottles of water, the man just cries!
Man at Airport "How did you know I was thirsty, I haven't had anything to drink for the last 8 hours because my flight was delayed and I fell asleep!"

Billy:
Oh I know Sir because my Father told me! (*And walks away, turns around and tells the man*) You don't have to worry about your daughter, Deborah, she was stuck in traffic, no accident okay! She'll be here in 10 minutes!
Man at airport how do you know my daughter? Who are you?
(*Lights out*)

SCENE 3

(*They get to the church, Miracle Temple where all the leaders are waiting for them*)

Pastor Frank:
So, so, Happy and blessed to have everyone here, we're going to have an anointed time together! Oh, and we welcome the young lad also, but it may become a little boring for you!
(*Billy just smiles and shakes his head!*)

Deacon Smith:
I have some scriptures to start off with…Acts chapter… (*Billy interrupts*)

Billy:
Excuse me Sir, but I believe we need to start off with prayer!
(*Everyone gets quiet, but they allow Him to Pray*)
He bows his head, lifts his hands and prays, Father, may your perfect will be done in us and through us, may your perfect ways be followed, and may your perfect words flow from us in your Holy name Amen!

Deacon Smith:
(*under his breath*)
Now just who does he think he is?
(*Billy walks over to him and gives him the last bottle of water and smiles at him*)
The weekend activities end, and everyone leaves having a grand time!

SCENE 4

The Joys: (*back home*)

Narrator
They return home, to Hinesville Georgia fully overjoyed, but exhausted and didn't even unpack their luggage! The next morning Annie calls for Billy to bring his dirty clothes to the washing machine, no answer so, she goes to his room!

Annie: (*yells*)
You better get up now and do what I say!
(*goes to his room but his room is empty they realized that Billy is nowhere to be found*) She calls the church in a panic, asking if their son was there. (*Elder Moore answers*)

Elder Moore:
Hello Sis Annie, why of course Billy is still here, he's been having some fired up meetings with Pastor Frank, Deacon Smith and anyone who wants to listen! As a matter of fact, here is Deacon Smith now!

Deacon Smith:
Hello Sis Annie, Billy is doing fine, and we thought you guys knew he was here since he hasn't shown any fear about being here! Plus, he even walked through the church and prayed for every room! He laid hands on me and I'll never be the same t was like a warm heat flowing through my body, I almost shouted!

Annie Joy:
That's all good Sir, but you better send my son home on the next plane! By the way, put him on this phone right now!

Billy Joy:
Hello mother, I am doing well and remember that wherever I go I have to be about my Father's Business!! I'll be home sometime hopefully, before midnight. I love you and daddy! Bye now I have to talk to Evangelist Lovely on the true meaning of forgiveness which makes her totally free!

Evangelist Lovely:
Yes Sis Annie, I thank God for your son because I have been dealing with an unruly, rebellious teenager and I was about to send her to her aunts' house for the next two years, until she graduates high school! But Billy reminded me of the prodigal son in the Bible how he came to himself and realized his foolishness!

Annie Joy: (*softly answers*)
God's will be done! Amen! Tell my son I will see him tomorrow ok and that I love him very much! (*Hangs up*)

Larry Joy:
You know we better get used to this; he is a special child and always goes around praying and encouraging people. We don't want to ever be embarrassed. So, we just always have to be sure he has an extra pack of clean socks and underwear wherever we go! (*They both look at each other, laughing*) Saying...Amen!

Jesus Birth in our Technology World!

Cast of Characters

Mary	Young pregnant teenager
Joseph	Mary's boyfriend
Dr Luke	Obstetrician/Medical Dr.
God's Voice	Speaks over microphone
Mary's Mother	God fearing Christian
Mary's Father	Strict disciplinarian
Ryan	Irritating young neighbor
Elisabeth	Cousin in New York
Louis Blessings	Taxi Driver
Mitchell Priest	Governor of NY
Officer Bishop	Police Commissioner
Lana Trusting	News Reporter
A.J. Glory	Anchorman WWJD News

Three Kings well dressed

- 1st King has a digital camera with 500 shares of Facebook stock.
- 2nd King has 1 bag of gold
- 3rd King has a pile of silk material

Props needed for each scene
Scene 1- HOPE
• 2 chairs, one table, doctor office, doctor's chart • 2 microphones • Part B of scene 1: Motorcycle sound effects, outside setting, helmet
Scene 2-PEACE
• 3 chairs for living room setting • Table with bible and large candle • 3 microphones, motorcycle helmet, and baseball bat
Scene 3-JOY
• (Sound affects) La Guardia Airport noise with plane taking off in background, Flight announcements • 4 Chairs set up for a taxi ride • 3 microphones, one carryon luggage bag • A sign with Mary, Joseph, Elisabeth name printed in bold letters

Scene 4- LOVE
- Badges for news reporter, and police commissioner
- Cell phones/tablets
- Flashing lights
- (Sound affects) helicopter sound, loudspeaker/megaphone 4 microphones

HOPE SCENE 1

(Mary is sitting at the doctor office waiting for the doctor. She is texting on her cell phone when the doctor enters)

Dr. Luke:
Hello Mary, I am so glad you could come in at such a short notice, its urgent that I saw you today.

Mary:
Oh no problem Dr. Luke, how are you doing?

Dr. Luke:
I am great! The major question is, how are you?

Mary:
Oh I'm fine, but what do you mean by that, is there something wrong with me? Did my labs come back abnormal? I don't know why I've been gaining a little weight in my stomach area; I eat healthy.

Dr. Luke:
Well I can tell you the reason, because you're pregnant!

Mary:
Oh no sir, that's not possible! No Way! I am still a VIRGIN! *(Shaking head and hands)*

Dr. Luke:
If you say so, but you are still very pregnant.

Mary:
Oh okay then that explains those text messages I've been receiving every morning around 3 am. Dr. this may sound crazy, but I honestly tell you that I've been receiving texts from someone named Gabriel! He says he's a guy that's an angel! I don't know him, never heard of him but he knows me, knows where I live, my name, my church, my age even my boyfriend's name! He keeps telling me that I am favored by God and will conceive a baby! Of course, I thought it was a prank.

Dr. Luke:
OOOO... okay! Look I know you're scared and nervous about this, but all I can do for you is set up your appointments and start you on the prenatal vitamins. Now according to the law, I also need to get in touch with your parents and let them know about this, do you understand?

Mary:
Yes sir I do, and I'd rather have you tell them before I do, maybe they'll just join hands and pray, and then once I tell them it won't be as bad!

Dr. Luke:
Well let me get the prescription, and a free bottle to start on, I'll be right back. (*Doctor leaves the room*)

Mary: (*Calls boyfriend on cell, hysterically*)
Hey, I need to see you ASAP! Please meet me in Excel Church parking lot off Phillips Hwy in about 30 minutes and I am not playing, you better be there or else! It's an emergency; life or death...YOURS!

Dr. Luke: (R*eturns to the room holding the bottle of vitamins*)
Oh I see you called your boyfriend? That's smart since he has a part in this too. Tell him the truth and don't be afraid. Here are your vitamins and your next appointment, you will also have to have lab work done in the next week. (*Hands her the papers*)
(*Lights out*)

PART B SCENE 1

(*Sound effects: Loud Motorcycle. Mary and Joseph meet in parking lot area*)

Joseph:
Mary what's wrong, what's going on with you? You sounded so upset! Are you okay?

Mary:
No I am not okay Joseph, I am Pregnant!

Joseph:
What? Oh No way! I have never even kissed you! And all those hugs don't make a baby! Well, how could you do this to me? You better get a DNA test and see who the father is.

Mary:
Oh I know who the father is! I've been receiving text messages from some angel guy named Gabriel and he told me I was favored by God and that I was going to carry a child, a baby boy! This is a divine plan and we're a part of it.

Joseph:
Well, uh…uh God hasn't told me anything about all of this, I love you and was going to marry you! I wanted to but now this, my goodness! (*His cell phone rings*) Hello….hello

God:

Hi Joseph...do not fear! I am God! Don't freak out okay. It is true that Mary is carrying my redemption plan for man and I want you to relax and follow my instructions, do you understand?

Joseph:

Yes...yes Sir, I hear you, (*drops phone...mouth hangs open in shock...starts shaking...he looks at Mary and they both hold each other*)

PEACE SCENE 2

(*Mary is sitting at home waiting for her parents to come in from work, as they enter, she excitedly begins to talk*)

Mary:

Guess what mom? Guess what dad! I have some really great, miraculous, fantastic news to share!

Mother: (*interrupts*)
Oh, I bet I know what it is...You won something, right? A car? Some money? A family cruise? Wait...wait is it a new house?

Mary: (*laughing*)
No mom none of those, something way greater! I need you guys to sit down please. Well I am pregnant! (*While rubbing stomach*) I am going to have a baby boy; he was placed in my womb by the Holy Spirit!

Father: (*looks at the mother eye to eye*)
That is YOUR daughter talking! And you better do something with her quick!

Mother:
Lord, help me to breathe and count to 10….1….2…3…10! How in the world can you be pregnant? Don't you know what this means? (*Shaking her head*) why Lord, why is this happening to our family?

Father:
Call that Joseph boy and tell him he has 90 seconds to get over here or I'll come to get him! Do it now Mary.

Mary:
Mom, dad, just listen a minute please! (*Doorbell rings*) wow that was fast!

Ryan: (*runs in holding his cell phone*)
Hey Mary, you're gonna have a baby which means that you're in T…R…O…U…B..L..E! My mom sent me over here to tell you that you are not allowed to hang out with my sister, Purity anymore and I can take a picture to send out to FB, Instagram, Twitter, YouTube and Periscope (*holds up camera*) clicks picture laughing everybody knows what you did!

Mother:
Go home child and tell your mama I will meet her at 5:15 (*holds up both fists*)
(*Ryan runs out as the sound of a motorcycle is heard; Joseph runs in with his helmet in his hand*)

Joseph:
I got here as quick as I could, what's going on? (*Everyone sits down but Joseph*)

Mother:
Way too much is going on today. I won't be able to show my face in this city, Jacksonville will never be the same, north side, south side, east side, west side my daughter is the gossip of Winn Dixie, Publix, and Wal-Mart! (*Shakes her head crying out loudly*)

Mary:
Gee mom, sorry for the major embarrassment!

Father:
Well son, what do you have to say about all of this? I'm all ears; my .357magnum is in the safe so you've got time to talk.

Joseph:
Sir I received a phone call from GOD, he assured me that this is all His doing! None of mine! Honestly sir, I have never, ever, touched Mary, not even kissed, well I did kiss her hands and cheek once but that is all, I swear!

Father:
I guess we need to come up with a plan on how to handle this.

Joseph:
Excuse me sir, ma-am, the Lord has a plan that's better than mans' and I intend to follow His leading!

Mother:
OOH so now you're a smarty mouth? Well I have a plan too… (*Pulls out baseball bat from under chair, Joseph puts his hands up to protect his face*)

Father:
Hold on, wait a minute, maybe she just needs to get away from here, this city, and Jacksonville shoot the whole state of Florida! Probably better to go stay with family up north for a while, at least until the baby is born.

Mary:
That'll be great! I just saw on Facebook last week that auntie Elisabeth is 6 months pregnant. I could stay with her and Uncle Zacharias until the baby is born, that way the shameful talk will wear off you and mom.

Father:
Okay it's settled, Joseph is going with you and we'll get you both a one-way ticket to Mount Vernon New York tomorrow afternoon. You better pray that the Lord has some serious instructions for you young man!

Mary:
Sounds good to me, I'll start packing but I will only take one suitcase.

Joseph:
Well okay I guess I'll pack one carry-on bag too and take all my money out of my savings acct, it's only $1000 but it should help us get started.

Father: (*laughing*)
Son you're going to New York not Middleburg FL. You'll need much more than that and all of God's supernatural help, but since this is His business, I trust Him and pray that you keep your cell phone charged.

Mother:
Well God is real; He does still perform miracles and I do believe that Mary is telling the truth; anyway if you guys are lying the Lord will deal with you something fierce. (*Lights go out*)

JOY SCENE 3

(*Sounds effects-La Guardia airport noise, flight announcements, etc. Mary sees Elisabeth and they greet one another with hugs and kisses on the cheek*)

Mary:
Oh it's so good to see you! Wow, you're really out there what a blessing indeed!

Elisabeth:
Oh my dear you're just as blessed, I'm still amazed that I finally conceived, I'm no spring chicken you know, nether is Zacharias, funny how God does things sometimes.

Mary:
Joseph went to the men's room you would think he's the pregnant one sometimes, (*places hand on her stomach*) the baby just moved!

Elisabeth:
Oh my goodness so did mine; he just leaped in my womb (*rubs stomach*) I think they know each other already. (*Both ladies laugh*)

Taxi Driver: (*Taxi driver walks up to them holding a sign with all their names on it*)
Excuse me ladies, greetings to you, Mary, Elisabeth and a man named Joseph is supposed to be with you. I have been assigned to take you to Luke Chapter One Drive.

Elisabeth:
Hey who are you? How do you know our names and my address?

Joseph: (*Joseph comes in the group*)
Hi sir, you're just the one I got a call about a few minutes ago, and I see you have the sign with our names spelled correctly, (*turns to the ladies*) he's safe no worries.

Taxi Driver:
No need to fear Ms. Elisabeth, I am on a special assignment from the Master, Yeshua (*a news reporter lady with a camera comes up to take pictures and salutes them*)

Mary:
Hey that's the same lady who was on the plane, sitting behind us and she just kept starring and smiling, I think she's following us! It doesn't matter.

Joseph: (*As they prepare to get in the Taxi, Joseph loads the bags in the back trunk and sits up front with the driver*)
I know they gonna talk the whole ride so we better get prepared for it. This is going to be the longest 20 minutes ever!

Mary:
So how is Zacharias taking this shock of a pregnancy? Is he shouting about it everywhere he goes?

Elisabeth:
Well not really, you see he didn't believe the angel Gabriel that came to him once while he was praying and told him, he hasn't spoken a word since! Just like a man. You know we would've posted it on social media in 5 seconds! I must say I find this truly fascinating; here I am 62 years old and pregnant!

Mary:
Oh yes, it is a miracle! I wish I could stay for the birth of your son, but we can only be here about 2 months, I received the text last night and Joseph received it also. We have to be in Times Square, the birthing has to take place there.

Elisabeth:
Well, all we can do is trust and obey right?

Taxi Driver:
By the way, do you have a name for the baby? You must be careful about the name since it will follow him his entire life.

Mary: (*Mary interrupts*)
Of course he has a name; he will be named after his father, Zacharias, right Elisabeth?

Joseph:
I know my son is gonna be named by Yeshua and it really doesn't bother me. Hopefully, Zacharias will be happy having a junior.

Elisabeth:
Oh he's already ticked off; he hasn't spoken one word since his angelic encounter that told him our sons' name our son shall be named...John! (*Lights go off*)

LOVE SCENE 4

Joseph: (*Sitting somewhere in Times Square dials #*)
Hello this is Joseph and I am supposed to call this number and ask for Governor Mitchell Priest.

Governor:
Yes Sir Mr. Joseph, I've been waiting on your call. How may I assist you with the birth of your baby? How is Mary and where are you guys?

Joseph:
Well I am not sure where we are, we walked on a street named Eighth Avenue, this morning, and we have been to the Hilton Inn, Ramada Inn, Holiday Inn, Sheraton, Comfort Suites, La Quinta Inn and no one has any vacancies. We've been here for three days now and slept in Central park. I am curious about one thing; how do you know us?

Governor:
All I can tell you is that Yeshua has a divine plan for you, Mary and your baby. I was to prepare Times Square for your safe delivery, but you see how congested the traffic is due to the holidays. I have been ordered to get you to Sheep Meadow around the Central Park Area.

Joseph:
This city is extremely busy, do people ever sleep? I don't know what to do or where to go so I am at your mercy, we're hungry and tired, Mary is soon to deliver; she told me she only has about 8 hours to go!

Governor:
No worries I am sending our helicopter to pick you up, I have you on our phone finder tracker and will have you in the designated area within an hour, just listen and follow directions alright.
(Sound effects of helicopter and megaphone announcing) "WARNING STAY 5 MILES OUT FROM THE SHEEP MEADOW AREA IN CENTRAL PARK! ALL NORTH, SOUTH, EAST, AND WEST

ENTRYWAYS ARE BLOCKED! BARICADES ARE PLACED FOR THE NEXT 24 HOURS. ALL TOURS ARE CANCELLED. THIS SHUT DOWN STARTS AT 1 PM TODAY AND CONTINUES UNTIL 1 PM TOMORROW GOVERNOR PRIEST THANKS YOU FOR YOUR COMPLIENCE."

(*This is also repeated once Mary and Joseph are safe at their destination*)

Mary: (*Joseph and Mary prepare to board helicopter; the news reporter appears and snaps another picture as they board*)

This is too overwhelming for me; I wish I could just go to sleep and wake up with the baby in my arms!

(Sound effects continue with helicopter and announcement)
"ALL CITIZENS STAY CLEAR 5 MILES FROM CENTRAL PARK"

(*Mary and Joseph settle down in the park and get ready for the baby's birth*)

Anchorman: (*News crew is set and trying to gather information*) As we can see, no one is allowed beyond the 5-mile barriers we're not sure what's going on, but reports are coming in from Times Square ticker news that a miracle is taking place! The entire area is as serene as ever and I have the Police commissioner Priest here live with an astounding report.

Commissioner:
I can't explain this! We have had no crimes committed in the last 72 hours, not one! Every precinct reports the same thing. We got word about a man named Joseph and his fiancée Mary being in the Central Park area; they came to the city 3 days ago! All the animals at the zoo went to sleep once they stepped on the property and they've been sleeping since! The Zoo

managers can't explain any of it, but all the animals are doing fine. Whatever they brought with them is having an incredibly peaceful & positive effect on our entire population, even the taxi drivers are taking people to their destinations free of charge!

Anchorman:
Breaking News Report!!!
We now have Lana Trusting with our W.W.J.D. news crew live at the Sheep Meadow area, Central Park, what's happening Lana?

Lana:
Well A.J. we have heard this piercing, loud cry of an infant and it seems like Mary has had the baby! Also, there was a huge bright star in the sky that appeared right over the area, we captured a picture of it and will show it to our viewers later. Also, there are three businessmen dressed in Stuart Hughes Diamond Edition Suits! WOW! Oh sorry, A.J. But they were able to walk right through the barriers somehow and the police didn't even see them, talk about weird!

Anchorman:
I've just received a report from Deliverance City Hospital's head OB/GYN, Dr. Luke and he says that his medical team performed every test known but they couldn't come up with a match for the DNA, also they stated that Mary's hymen was not broken!

Lana:
Thousands of people are lining up from the 5-mile marker to get a glimpse of the spectacular event. Nobody wants to leave without seeing this "Miracle Baby" I know I'm going to go get in line too. Lana Trusting reporting W.W.J.D. news back at you A.J.

Anchorman:
Thanks Lana, it looks like this could very well be….THE GREATEST STORY EVER HAPPENED IN NY This is A.J. Glory with your evening news from W.W.J.D, Times Square NY.

(*Joseph, Mary and Baby are on the lawn*)
Mary:
You know his name is to be Jesus okay!

Joseph:
Yes, I know, it is well

Three businessmen walk up to them; they each present their gift to the baby, never saying a word!
- The first one bows and presents a Cannon Diamond Plus digital camera and 500 shares of Facebook stock
- The second one bows and presents a bag of gold coins
- The third one bows and presents silk material

Mary and Joseph (both say)
WELCOME TO THE WORLD BABY JESUS!!! WE LOVE YOU!!!
(Lights out end of play)

Staying in Your Lane, Keeps You Sane

I believe in life we sow to grow
and we give to live.
Every day we're giving something away,
time, prayers, money, words,
they're all seeds sown
They will produce a harvest full-grown.
People often respond and react based on their season in life,
yet we can combat it by checking to see if our season is of peace
or strife

It's okay to say, "no" with a smile on your face,
that's one way of showing the beauty of God's grace!
But too often we lie just to please someone else
While deeply inside frustrating yourself.
It's safe to complain to the one who reigns
but much wiser to stay true to yourself,
staying in your lane
to keep yourself sane!
Amen

About the Author

Venasta was born and raised in Knoxville, TN and endured life as a foster child. She was blessed to be the mother of the "fantastic four", two sons and two daughters. She was a proud, United States Army Veteran and a born-again Christian; not religious but relational.

Venasta decided to write this book after becoming a Guardian Ad Litem, Court Appointed Special Advocate for the states of Georgia and Florida. She thought about how her experience would make kids who she was assigned to feel more at ease and comfortable as she built and laid a foundation of trust.

Venasta started journaling in 2014. She was inspired by knowing others will see, feel, and understand that real life happens to all of us. We just learn how to continue with tears, laughter, and prayer! She truly believes there are a few more books within her to tell life's story from a real perspective because we live in a real world.

Venasta is finally believing, receiving, and living a daily, supernaturally satisfied, married, life with her husband Joseph in Jacksonville, FL.

www.ingramcontent.com/pod-product-compliance
Ingram Content Group UK Ltd.
Pitfield, Milton Keynes, MK11 3LW, UK
UKHW021304180426
11947UKWH00015B/1016